G000110008

© 2004 Feierabend Verlag OHG
Mommsenstr. 43, D-10629 Berlin

Originalausgabe:
© Gribaudo, Savigliano (Cn), Italien
edizioni.gribaudo@libero.it

Fotografische Beiträge – *Photographic Contributions*

Die meisten der im Band *Michael Schumacher* enthaltenen Bilder wurden von
Paolo D'Alessio gemacht oder gehören zu seinem persönlichen Archiv. Für die
weiteren Bilder dankt der Herausgeber:

*Most of the photographs contained in this book have been taken by Paolo
D'Alessio or belong to his personal archive. For the remaining photographs we
would like to thank:*

Actualfoto, Gherardo Benfenati, Kazuhiro Tajima, Bryn Williams.

Editor: Paola Morelli
Texte und technische Zeichnungen: Paolo D'Alessio
Deutsche Übersetzung: Diana Mecarelli für Durante & Zoratti, Köln
Englische Übersetzung: Julian Thomas
Lithografie: Gi.Mac, Savigliano (Cn)
Druck und Bindung: Grafiche Busti, Colognola ai Colli (Vr)

Printed in Italy
ISBN 3-89985-046-7
20 04074 1

Michael
Schumacher

Paolo D'Alessio

1994 2001
1995 2002
2000 2003

1994
1995
2000

2001

2002

2003

8

Die Geschichte
History

1991 Grand Prix von Belgien: Im Jordan-Ford mit der Nummer 32 tritt Michael Schumacher erstmals öffentlich auf. Der Deutsche fährt überraschend die siebent-beste Rundenzeit im Qualifying, eine Leistung, die ihm den direkten Wechsel zu Flavio Briatores Benetton-Team einbringt.

1991 Belgian GP: a certain Michael Schumacher makes his debut in the #32 Jordan-Ford. The German driver surprisingly sets seventh quickest time in qualifying, a performance that immediately earns him a switch to Flavio Briatore's Benetton team.

1992 Grand Prix von Belgien: Ein Jahr nach seinem Debüt gewinnt Michael Schumacher den ersten Grand Prix seiner Karriere…

1992 Belgian GP: one year after his Formula 1 debut, Michael Schumacher wins the first Grand Prix race of his career…

9

1993 ... das gleiche Ergebnis erzielt er im Folgejahr im Grand Prix von Portugal. Am Ende der Saison ist Schumacher mit 52 Punkten Vierter in der Rangliste der Fahrer-WM, hinter Alain Prost, Ayrton Senna und Damon Hill.

1993 ... *a result he repeated the following year in the Portuguese GP. At the end of the season, with 52 points to his name, Schumacher finishes fourth in the Drivers' standings behind Alain Prost, Ayrton Senna and Damon Hill.*

1994 Erster, äußerst umstrittener Weltmeistertitel für Michael Schumacher am Steuer des Benetton-Ford, in der vom tragischen Tod Ayrton Sennas überschatteten Saison.

1994 *Michael Schumacher wins his first, controversial world title with Benetton-Ford in a season marred by the tragic death of Ayrton Senna.*

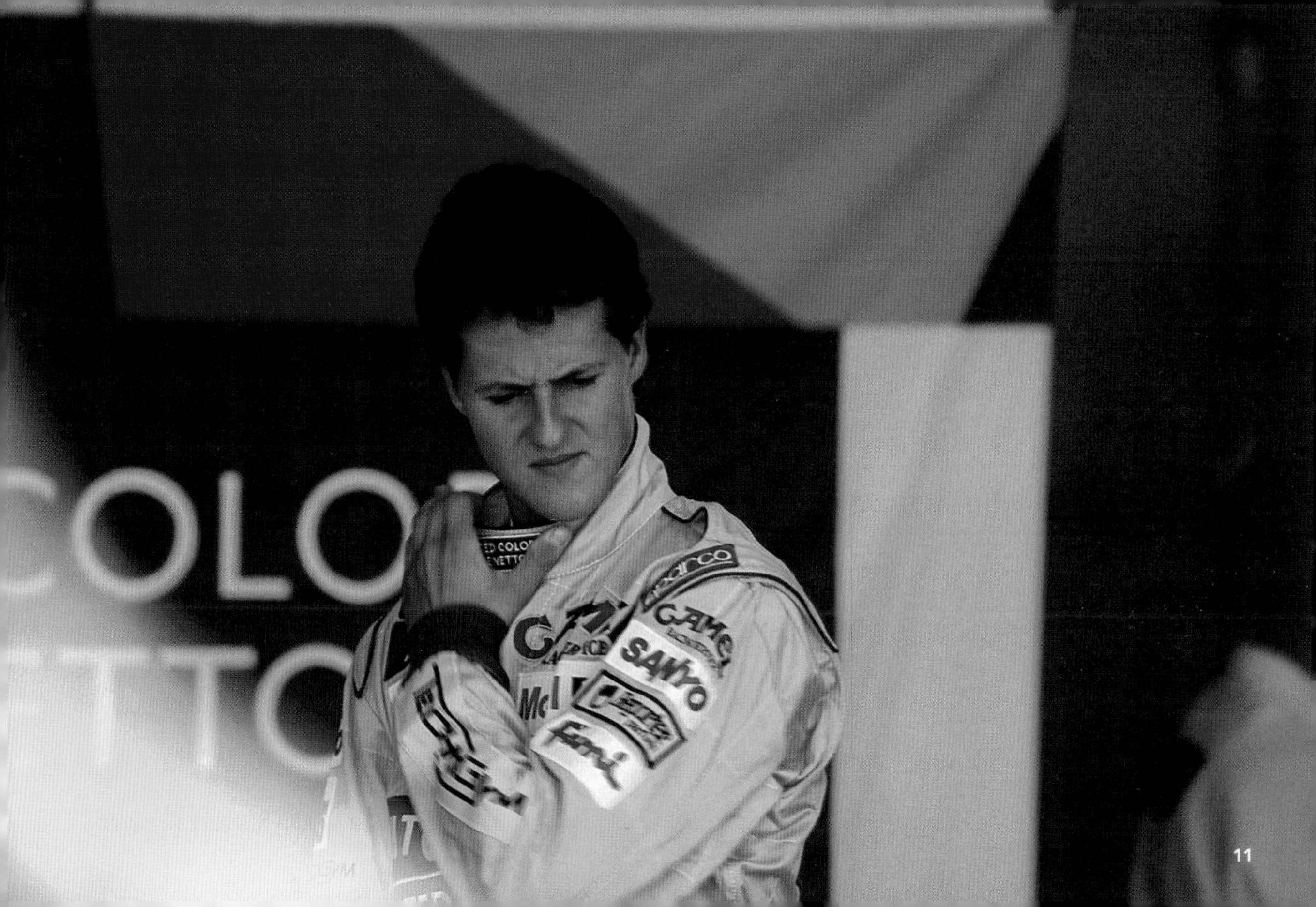
COLO
SANYO

13

1995 Benetton wechselt zum 10-Zylinder-Renault, und Schumacher behauptet sich als Weltmeister. Am Jahresende verlässt er das Team von Briatore und wird erster Fahrer bei Ferrari.

1995 Benetton switches to the ten-cylinder Renault engine and Schumacher wins the world title for the second time. At the end of the year he leaves Briatore's team for Ferrari.

1996 Schumacher schenkt den Fans vom "Cavallino" drei Siege (Spanien, Belgien und Italien), auch wenn der F310 sicher keines der Top-Fahrzeuge ist…

1996 - Schumacher wins three races for Ferrari (Spain, Belgium and Italy), even though the F310 is not one of the best cars on the track…

18

1997 In Jerez, dem letzten Rennen der Saison, vergibt Schumacher die Chance den Titel zu gewinnen, als er nur wenige Runden vor dem Ziel mit dem Williams-Renault von Jacques Villeneuve kollidiert.

1997 *At Jerez, in the final round of the season, Schumacher loses all chance of winning the title when he clashes with Jacques Villeneuve (Williams-Renault) just a few laps from the end.*

1998 Zwölf Monate danach, in Suzuka, wiederholt sich die Geschichte aufgrund eines platzenden Reifens, der den Piloten von Ferrari aus dem Rennen wirft.

1998 *Twelve months later, history repeats itself at Suzuka when a tyre explodes, putting paid to Schumacher's title chances.*

1999 Ein schrecklicher Unfall in Silverstone zwingt Schumacher einige Grand Prix auszusetzen. Trotzdem gewinnt Ferrari am Jahresende den Konstrukteurs-Weltmeistertitel.

1999 A horrific crash at Silverstone forces Schumacher to miss several races. Despite this, Ferrari wins the constructors' title at the end of the year.

2000-2003 Jüngste Geschichte, mit vier Weltmeisterschaften in ebenso vielen Saisons.

2000-2003 Recent history, with the conquest of four world titles in four seasons.

23

1994

Der erste von Michael Schumachers Weltmeistertiteln ist zweifellos der unsicherste, der umstrittenste, der kontroverseste in der gesamten Karriere des deutschen Fahrers. Eine hart erkämpfte WM, in einer furchtbaren, durch den Tod von Ayrton Senna erschütterten Saison, und gewonnen mit einem Fahrzeug, das nicht über jeden Verdacht erhaben war. Zuerst wird die Saison überraschend mit zwei Erfolgen des Kerpener Rennfahrers eröffnet, während die großen Titelfavoriten Williams-Renault und Ayrton Senna ohne Punkte ausgehen. Dann kommt die tragische Wende in Imola, als der brasilianische Weltmeister sein Leben infolge eines heftigen Crashs nach der Tamburello-Kurve verliert und Michael Schumacher automatisch sein Nachfolger wird. Der Deutsche enttäuscht die Erwartungen nicht. Aber obwohl er gewinnt, gewinnt er nicht überzeugend, weil sein Benetton-Ford unter dem Verdacht steht, verbotene elektronische Systeme zu verwenden.

Seinerseits tut Briatores Fahrer mit seinem aggressiven und dreisten Fahrstil alles, um die Polemik wieder anzufachen. Er handelt sich sogar eine Sperre von zwei Rennen ein, weil er im Grand Prix von England die schwarze Fahne ignoriert hat. Nicht weniger umstritten ist der Zwischenfall beim entscheidenden Grand Prix von Australien. Schumacher, offensichtlich in technischen Schwierigkeiten, verleitet Damon Hill zu einem Fehler. Die beiden stoßen zusammen und das Ausscheiden der beiden Fahrzeuge schenkt dem Deutschen den ersten Titel seiner Karriere.

1994

Michael Schumacher's first world title was undoubtedly the most uncertain, the most hard-fought and the most controversial in the German driver's career. It was a title he won by the skin of his teeth, in a dreadful season marred by the death of Ayrton Senna, and with a car that aroused considerable suspicion.

The season got underway with two wins for the Kerpen-born driver, while Ayrton Senna and Williams-Renault, the favourites for the title, finish out of the points. The tragic turning point came at Imola, when the Brazilian driver lost his life in a violent crash at the Tamburello, leaving Michael Schumacher automatically to take up the mantle as Formula 1's number 1 driver. The German did not fail to live up to expectations and although he won, he did not win convincingly, because his Benetton-Ford was suspected of using illegal electronic devices.

For his part Briatore's driver, with his aggressive and no-holds-barred driving style, did nothing to play down the controversy. The German was even forced to miss two races for ignoring a black flag in the British GP. The decisive Australian GP also aroused its fair share of controversy when Schumacher, who was clearly in crisis, forced Damon Hill into an error. The two drivers clashed and were out of the race, an incident that handed the German his first world title on a plate.

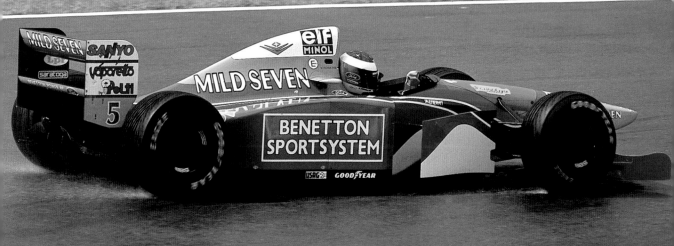

Michael Schumacher
(rechts, auf dem
Podium von San Paolo)
gewinnt überraschend
den Grand Prix von
Brasilien 1994, obwohl
das lokale Idol Ayrton
Senna und sein
Williams bis dahin als
Favoriten galten.

*Michael Schumacher
(alongside, on the
Sao Paulo podium)
surprisingly won
the 1994 Brazilian GP,
when local idol
Ayrton Senna
and his Williams
were considered
as favourites.*

29

Nach dem
tragischen Tod
von Ayrton Senna
im Grand Prix
von San Marino
wird Schumacher
(erneut Erster in
Imola) der
Spitzenpilot des
Formel-1-Zirkus.

*After the tragic
death of Ayrton
Senna in the
San Marino GP,
Schumacher (who
won at Imola)
became the
leading driver
in Formula 1.*

Ayrton Senna fährt in den ersten Runden des Grand Prix von San Marino vor Schumachers Benetton.

Ayrton Senna leads the Benetton of Schumacher in the opening laps of the San Marino GP.

Sennas Tod bewegte Schumacher zutiefst. Am Vorabend von Monte Carlo denkt der deutsche Rennfahrer sogar über seinen Rückzug aus dem Motorsport nach.

The death of Senna deeply disturbed Schumacher. Before the Monte Carlo race, the German driver was seriously considering retiring from motor sport.

Schumi gewinnt
sechs der ersten
sieben WM-
Rennen, indem
er sich in
Brasilien,
Aida, Imola,
Montecarlo,
Kanada und
Frankreich
behauptet.

*Schumy won six
of the first seven
rounds of the
championship,
in Brazil,
at Aida, Imola,
in Montecarlo,
Canada
and France.*

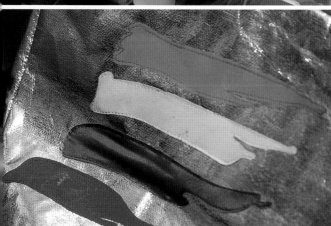

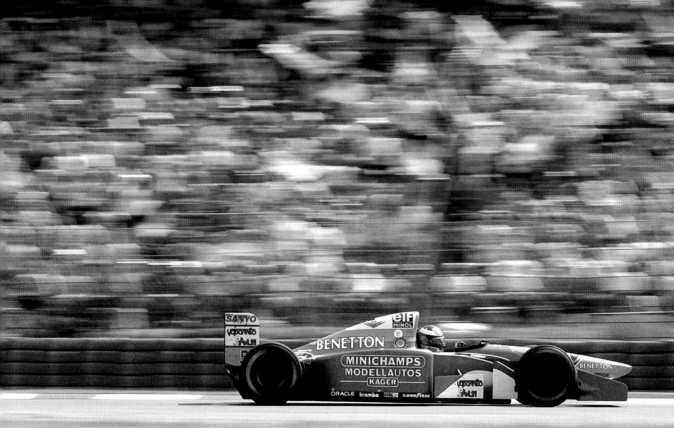

Nach der
Disqualifikation
Schumachers
durch die FIA
aufgrund der
Geschehnisse in
Silverstone wird
Damon Hill zum
gefährlichen
Gegner für die
WM '94.

*After the
disqualification
inflicted
by the FIA
on Schumacher
for the events
at Silverstone,
Damon Hill
became a rival
for the 1994
championship.*

43

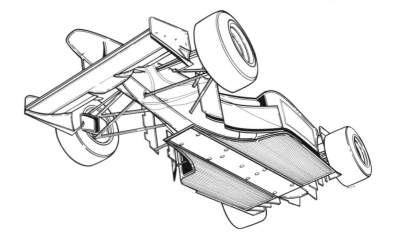

BENETTON-FORD B194

Der B194, mit dem er den ersten WM-Titel gewonnen hat.
Schumacher's Benetton B194 that won the first world title.

1995

Zum ersten Mal im Laufe seiner Karriere präsentiert sich Michael Schumacher am Start der neuen WM mit der Nummer Eins auf der Front seines Autos, wie es dem amtierenden Weltmeister zusteht. Eine Auszeichnung, die Enzo Ferrari einmal als "… der Abstiegsbeginn des Champions" bezeichnet hatte.

Bei Schumacher jedoch bewirkt dies den gegenteiligen Effekt. Dem Kerpener Rennfahrer reicht sein Titel von '94 nicht und er will der ganzen Welt beweisen, dass es sich nicht um ein Zufallsergebnis handelt, sondern um den ersten Meilenstein einer glorreichen Karriere. Benettons tut seinerseits alles, um ihm zu helfen. So werden die auch fähigen V8-Ford-Zetec-R-Motoren von 1994 durch Renaults stärkere 10-Zylinder-Motoren ersetzt. Es handelt sich um die gleichen Motoren, mit denen der Williams ausgestattet ist, die beträchtlich mehr PS haben und ein besseres Fahrverhalten. Mit der Leistungsfähigkeit des V10-Motors, der die technischen Schwächen des Benetton B195 etwas ausgleicht, sichert sich Schumacher den zweiten WM-Titel seiner Karriere mit neun Siegen und 102 Punkten in der Rangliste.

Am Ende der Saison jedoch kommt es aus heiterem Himmel zur Trennung von dem von Briatore geführten Rennstall. Von einem Mega-Vertrag angezogen und vielleicht durch einen Anstoß von Bernie Ecclestone persönlich, dem unangefochtenen Boss der Formel 1, verlässt Michael Schumacher Benetton, um zu Ferrari zu wechseln. Ziel: den Weltmeister-titel nach einer langen Durststrecke wieder nach Maranello zurückzuholen.

1995

For the first time in his career Michael Schumacher started a new world championship with the #1 plate on his car as reigning world champion. In the past Enzo Ferrari used to define this recognition as the start of '... the downward spiral of the champion'.

Instead it had the opposite effect on Schumacher. The driver from Kerpen was hardly satisfied with his 1994 title and wanted to show the entire world that the result had not come about by chance, but that it was the first tassel in a lustrous career.

For its part Benetton did everything possible to give him a hand, replacing the still valid V8 Ford Zetec-R engine from 1994 with the more powerful ten-cylinder Renault unit. This was the same engine that powered the Williams and guaranteed considerable extra horsepower, as well as better driveability. Schumacher exploited the potential of the French V10 engine to compensate for the technical weaknesses of the Benetton B195 to take the second world title of his career, with nine wins and 102 points to his name.

At the end of the season however Schumacher shocked the world when he left the squad directed by Flavio Briatore. Attracted by a lucrative contract and maybe even after a 'nudge' from Bernie Ecclestone, the undisputed boss of Formula 1, Michael Schumacher left Benetton to join Ferrari. The aim was to bring back the world title to Maranello after a lengthy absence.

Große Neuig-
keiten bei
Benetton im
Jahr 1995:
Der B195
erscheint mit
der Nummer
des Welt-
meisters auf
der Nase und
wird von
Renaults 10-
Zylinder-Motor
angetrieben.

*Benetton
presented
major changes
for 1995: the
B195 sported
the #1 plate
on its nose and
was powered
by Renault's
ten-cylinder
engine.*

Auch wenn der
Benetton B195
ein schwer
zu fahrender
Rennwagen
ist, fährt
Schumacher
mit ihm ganze
neun Mal zum
Erfolg.

*Even though
the Benetton
B195 was
a difficult car
to drive,
Schumacher
successfully
took it to the
chequered flag
on nine
occasions.*

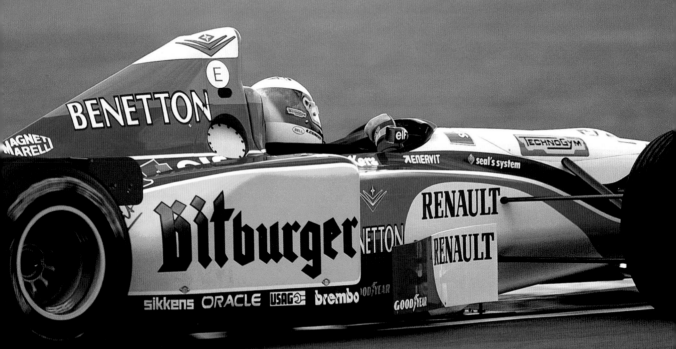

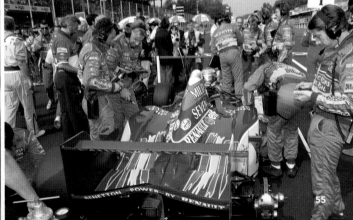

Auch '95 trifft
Schumacher auf
Damon Hill, den
Rennfahrer von
Williams-Renault,
der ihm den Sieg
bis zum Grand
Prix vom Pazifik
in Aida streitig
macht.

*Schumacher had
to fend off the
challenge from
Williams-Renault
driver Damon Hill
again in 1995.
Hill's challenge
went right down
to the final race,
the Pacific GP
at Aida.*

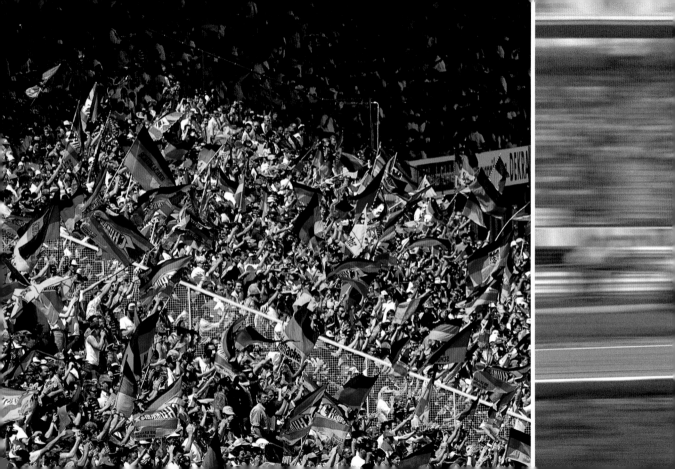

Im Sommer 1995 reift die aufsehen-erregende Trennung des amtierenden Weltmeisters von Benetton, begünstigt durch Bernie Ecclestone, der ein erfolgreiches Ferrari-Team in der F1 benötigt.

The summer of 1995 saw the beginning of the sensational divorce between the reigning world champion and Benetton, with the guiding hand of Bernie Ecclestone, who desperately needed a successful Ferrari team in F1.

61

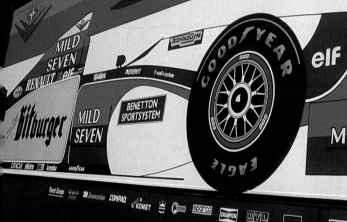

Benetton RENAULT
Racing Team

Benetton
Formula 1

MILD SEVEN
RENAULT elf
Bitburger
MILD SEVEN
BENETTON SPORTSYSTEM

TECHNOGYM
GOODYEAR 989
EAGLE

elf
MILD SEVEN
Lpr
MILD SEVEN

COMPAQ
KOMET
SPARCO
CHAMPION
RTL
EDS
EDS Unigraphics

UNITED COLORS
OF BENETTON.

62

MILD SEVEN

elf

SCHUMACHER
RENAULT F1

KicKers

ENERVIT

seal's system

TECHNOGYM

BEN
SPORTS

MILD SEVEN

RENAULT

RENAULT

urger
eer

USAG   brembo

GOOD YEAR

GOOD YEAR

Auf dem Podium von Aida feiern Flavio Briatore und Schumacher die Eroberung des zweiten Weltmeistertitels des deutschen Rennfahrers, der zum Jahresende zu Ferrari überwechseln wird.

On the Aida podium, Flavio Briatore and Schumacher celebrate the conquest of the second world title for the German, who left to join Ferrari at the end of the season.

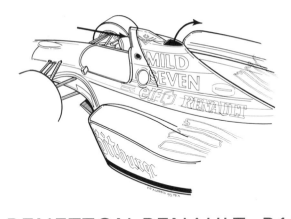

BENETTON-RENAULT B195

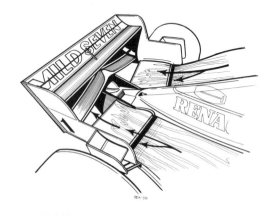

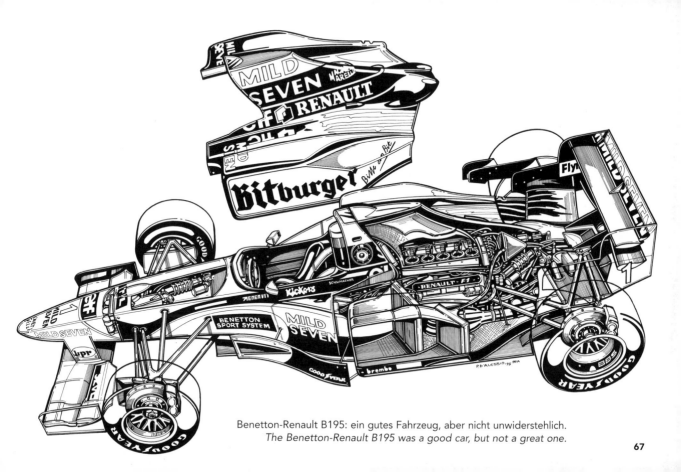

Benetton-Renault B195: ein gutes Fahrzeug, aber nicht unwiderstehlich.
The Benetton-Renault B195 was a good car, but not a great one.

Nach drei vergeblichen Anläufen (1997, 1998, 1999) gewinnt Michael Schumacher im Jahr 2000 endlich den dritten WM-Titel seiner Karriere und Ferrari kann nach einer 21-jährigen Durststrecke den Fahrertitel wieder für sich beanspruchen. Der letzte WM-Titel eines Ferrari-Fahrers geht mit dem Sieg des Südafrikaners Jody Scheckter auf 1979 zurück.

Den neun Saisonerfolgen zum Trotz (zehn Siege für Ferrari, mit dem Sieg von Barrichello in Deutschland) handelt es sich nicht um eine Spazierfahrt für den Ferrari-Fahrer. Nachdem er die erste Hälfte der Saison geführt hat (Schumacher ist Erster in Australien, Brasilien und Imola), wird dem Deutschen in Montecarlo Einhalt geboten. Grund hierfür war ein Defekt am Auspuff, der ihn zwingt, in der Endphase eines Rennens aufzugeben, in dem er bis zu diesem Moment geführt hat. Die Geschichte wiederholt sich in Frankreich und in Hockenheim, wo Schumacher, vom Motor seines Ferraris im Stich gelassen, gezwungen ist, das Handtuch zu werfen. Hiervon profitiert der amtierende Weltmeister, der Finne Mika Häkkinen, der nach dem Rennen in Spa zur Spitze der Rangliste aufsteigt. Schumacher lässt sich jedoch nicht entmutigen und kehrt mit dem Grand Prix in Italien ins Rampenlicht zurück. Unterstützt durch ein Fahrzeug, das wieder zuverlässig und konkurrenzfähig ist, triumphiert er in Monza und im Grand Prix in den USA, der zum ersten Mal auf der Rennstrecke von Indianapolis gefahren wird. In Suzuka, Japan, wird die Jagd auf den Weltmeistertitel mit einem Sieg gekrönt, der für ihn und Ferrari wie verhext zu sein schien.

After three unsuccessful attempts (1997, 1998 and 1999), in 2000 Michael Schumacher finally won his third world title and above all Ferrari could once again claim the Drivers' crown after a 21-year gap. The last world title won by a Ferrari driver dated back to 1979 with victory for South African Jody Scheckter.

Despite nine wins (ten in total, with Barrichello's in Germany), it was not all plain sailing for Schumacher. After dominating the first half of the season (with wins in Australia, Brazil and at Imola), the German was brought down to earth at Monte Carlo when a broken exhaust caused him to retire in the final stages of a race he had dominated from the start. The story was repeated in France and at Hockenheim, where Schumacher had to retire with engine problems on his Ferrari.

The reigning world champion, Finland's Mika Hakkinen, took advantage of Schumacher's crisis and moved into the lead of the championship after the Spa-Francorchamps race. The German however kept a cool head and returned to his early-season form from the Italian GP onwards. Backed up by a reliable and competitive Ferrari, Schumacher won at Monza and in the United States GP, which was held at the Indianapolis circuit for the first time. Then in Suzuka, he was finally able to wipe out what was becoming a jinx for himself and Ferrari by winning the world title.

Die WM im Jahr 2000 wird mit dem Sieg von Michael Schumacher und seinem Ferrari F1 2000 im GP von Australien eröffnet. Rechts der Deutsche auf dem Podium mit seinem neuen Ferrari-Teamkollegen Barrichello.

The 2000 championship got underway with a win for Michael Schumacher and his Ferrari F1 2000 in the Australian GP. Alongside, the German on the podium with his new Ferrari team-mate, Rubens Barrichello.

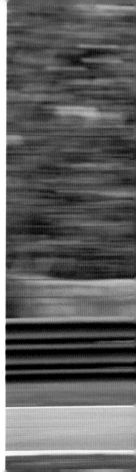

Nach Australien und Brasilien ist Imola an der Reihe. Mit dem Sieg bei Ferraris Heimrennen macht Schumacher einen entscheidenden Schritt in Richtung Weltmeistertitel in der WM der Formel 1 im Jahr 2000.

After Australia and Brazil, it was the turn of Imola. In winning Ferrari's home Grand Prix, Schumacher took a major step forward towards clinching the 2000 Formula 1 world title.

Die Ferrari-
Mechaniker
entfernen sich
von Schumachers
F1 2000 und der
deutsche Cham-
pion startet von
den Boxen nach
einem weiteren
Rekordzeit-
Boxenstopp.

*The Ferrari
mechanics move
away from
Schumacher's
F1 2000 and the
German champion
powers away
again after
another rapid
pit-stop.*

Schumachers Ferrari mit qualmenden Reifen beim Start des Grand Prix von Frankreich. Unten: der Deutsche in Aktion.

Schumacher's Ferrari wheel-smokes away at the start of the French GP. Above, the German in action.

89

Das Herz der Fans vom "Cavallino" schlägt für Michael Schumacher, den Superchampion aus Kerpen (seitlich).

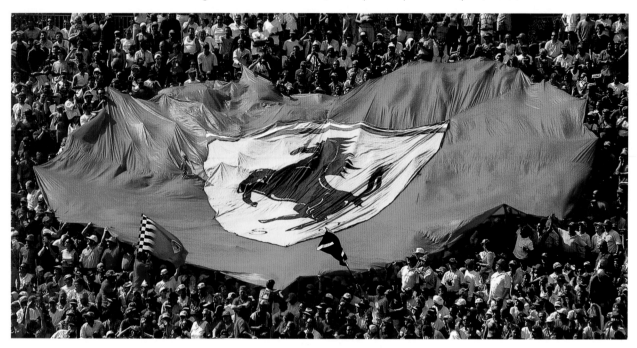

The heart of the Prancing Horse tifosi beats for Michael Schumacher, the champion from Kerpen (alongside).

SAP
UNITED STA
GRAND PRIX
INDIANAPOLIS 2000

SAP UNITED STATES GRAND PRIX
INDIANAPOLIS 2000

Der erste Platz im
Grand Prix von
Japan, in Suzuka
(seitlich), schenkt
Schumi die dritte
Weltmeisterschaft
seiner Karriere und
Italien gewinnt
den ersten
Fahrertitel seit '79.

*First place in the
Japanese GP at
Suzuka (alongside)
gives Schumacher
the third world
crown of his career
and brings back
the Driver's title
to Italy for the first
time since 1979.*

FERRARI F1 2000

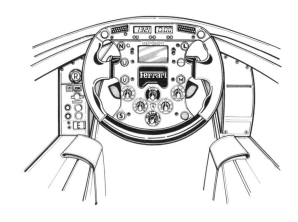

Die F1 2000 gewinnt zehn Grand Prix im Jahr 2000.
Unten das Lenkrad-Armaturenbrett.
The F1 2000 won ten races in 2000.
Below on the left the steering-wheel/display unit.

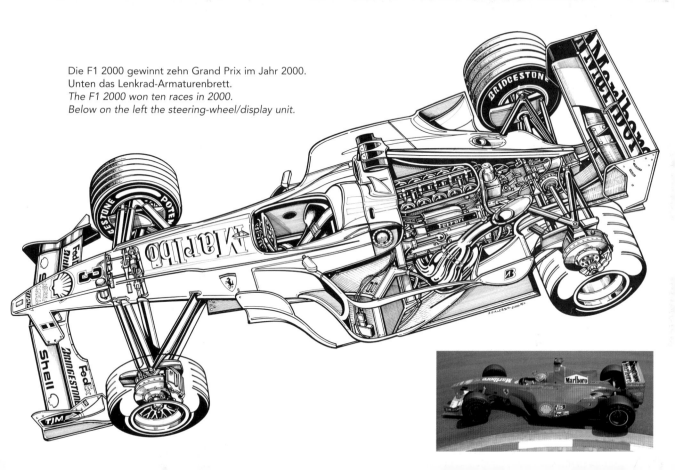

Die erste Weltmeisterschaft des neuen Jahrtausends beginnt mit neuen technischen FIA-Reglements, die dazu dienen sollen, die Geschwindigkeit der Fahrzeuge zu drosseln und den Abtrieb zu vermindern. Viele sind der Meinung, dass diese Regeln außerdem einen gewissen Ausgleich im Rennbetrieb der Formel 1 schaffen und die im Finale der Saison 2000 deutlich gezeigte Überlegenheit Ferraris verringern sollten. Aber genau das Gegenteil tritt ein. Wer nach der Serie von Siegen und WM-Titeln ein Nachlassen beim Team von Maranello und seinem Spitzenpiloten erwartet hatte, wird nun eines Besseren belehrt.

Und das wird sofort beim ersten Rennen der Saison klar, dem Grand Prix von Australien. Eine Tradition fortsetzend, die 1999 mit dem F399 begann, führt das Duo Schumacher-Ferrari vom Start an und besiegt die Konkurrenz. Nicht nur, dass Ferrari keinen Formverlust erkennen lässt, sondern, sofern dies überhaupt möglich ist, der neugeborene F2001 ist sogar besser als das Fahrzeug im Jahr 2000, und unter allen Spitzenfahrzeugen ist es dasjenige, das dem neuen technischen Reglement am besten angepasst ist.

Trotz des Fehlschlags in Imola, wo Schumacher zur Aufgabe gezwungen ist und Barrichello nur Dritter wird, verwandelt sich die Fortsetzung der Saison 2001 für die Roten und ihren Champion in einen langen Triumphzug. Insgesamt erlangt Kaiser Schumi neun Siege, und in Ungarn, vier Rennen vor Ende der WM, feiert der deutsche Rennfahrer den vierten Titel seiner Karriere und erreicht damit den Rekord von Alain Prost.

The first world championship of the new millennium got underway with new regulations introduced by the FIA, which aimed to slow down the cars and decrease downforce. Many observers thought that these rules would bring about a re-equilibrium of the Formula 1 grid and reduce Ferrari's clear superiority but they produced the exact opposite.

The Maranello-based team and its #1 driver had failed to be satisfied by the series of wins and world titles in 2000 and were out for more victories.

This was clear right from the opening round of the season, the Australian GP. Continuing a tradition that had begun in 1999 with the F399, the Schumacher-Ferrari partnership dominated right from the start and annihilated the opposition. Not only did Ferrari not show any drop in competitive form, but the new F2001 proved to be superior than the 2000 model in all respects and was the car that adapted the best to the new regulations.

After a poor result at Imola, where Schumacher was forced to retire and Barrichello could only finish third, the rest of the 2001 season turned into a non-stop triumphant cavalcade for the red cars and their champion. 'Kaiser Michael' picked up nine wins, and in Hungary, four rounds before the end of the championship, the German driver celebrated the fourth world title of his career, equalling Alain Prost's record.

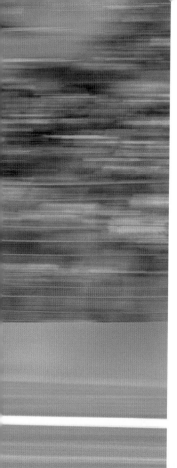

Jeder, der glaubte, Schumi sei demotiviert und Ferrari im Abstieg, muss seine Meinung ändern. 2001 sind der deutsche Rennfahrer und sein Roter immer noch das Paar, das geschlagen werden muss.

Anyone who thought that Schumacher was lacking in motivation and Ferrari was on a downward spiral had to think again. In 2001 the German driver and the Italian cars were once again the pairing to beat.

Marlboro

1

Shell

MAGNETI
MARELLI

FIAT

FedEx   FedEx

BRIDGESTONE   BRIDGESTONE

Shell   Shell

104

Einige technische Neuerungen des Ferrari F2001, wie die löffelförmigen Frontflügel, machen Schule und ermöglichen Schumacher die Saison 2001 zu dominieren.

Certain technical innovations on the Ferrari F2001, such as the 'spoon-shaped' front wing were avant-guard and allowed Schumacher to dominate the 2001 season.

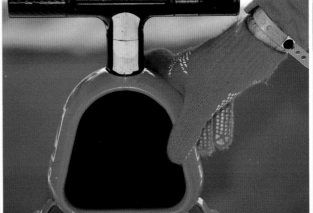

Fünf erste Plätze
im Grand Prix
von Monte Carlo
machen aus
Schumacher den
unbestrittenen
'König' des
Fürstentums. Auf
den Abbildungen
nimmt er die enge
Kurve des Loews.

*Five wins in the
Monaco GP
made Schumacher
the undisputed
'King' of the
Principality.
In the photos,
Schumacher
tackles the Loews
hairpin.*

Michael Schumacher nach dem x-ten Sieg von den Medien umringt. Auf den folgenden Seiten feiert er seinen Bruder Ralf, Erster in Kanada.

Michael Schumacher surrounded by media after yet another win. On the following pages, celebrating his brother Ralf, who won in Canada.

Michael Schumacher, Rubens Barrichello und Jean Todt (unten) feiern den Gewinn des doppelten Weltmeistertitels 2001 auf dem Podium des Grand Prix von Ungarn.

Michael Schumacher, Rubens Barrichello and Jean Todt (above) celebrate their 2001 double world title triumph on the Hungarian GP podium.

Ein ungewöhn-
liches Bild (links):
In Monza, nach
den tragischen
Geschehnissen
vom elften
September,
präsentiert Ferrari
seinen Boliden
ohne Sponsoring
und mit einer
schwarzen Nase
zum Zeichen
der Trauer.

*An unusual image
(on the left): at
Monza, after the
tragic events of
September 11th,
Ferrari sported a
sponsor-free
livery and a black
nosecone as a
sign of mourning.*

Ein eindringliches Porträt und eine Nahaufnahme vom vierfachen Weltmeister Michael Schumacher.

An intense portrait and a close-up of four-times world champion Michael Schumacher.

FERRARI F2001

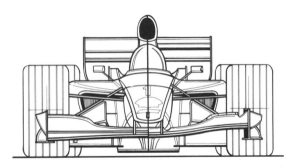

Der F2001, die Weiterentwicklung des Modells 2000, hat eine andere
Aerodynamik, Gewichtsverteilung und einen 90°-V10-Motor.

*The F2001, an evolution of the 2000 model, had a different
aerodynamic package, weight distribution and a 90° V10 engine.*

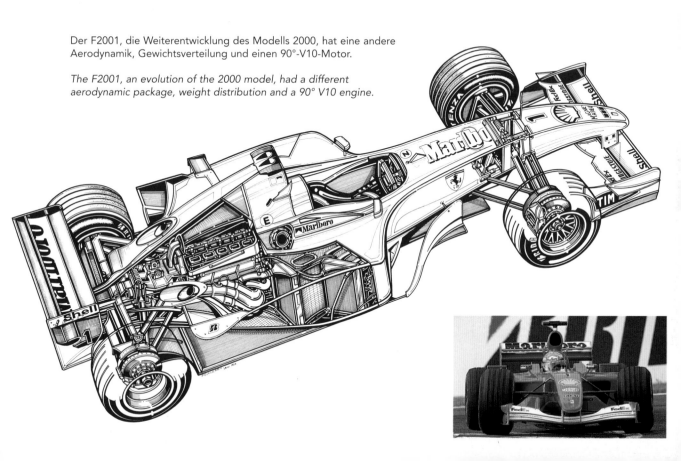

Ferrari überraschte alle, als sie mit dem Wagen von 2001 in die Saison 2002 starten, während sich der revolutionäre F2002 noch in der Fertigstellung befindet. Das Ergebnis bleibt jedoch das gleiche: Die Roten dominieren im Qualifying für den Grand Prix von Australien und Schumacher hat im Rennen mal wieder keine Gegner. So beginnt die WM der Rekorde für das Gespann Ferrari-Schumacher: Der deutsche Rennfahrer erweist sich als bester Formel-1-Fahrer, die Roten von Maranello beweisen ihre technische Überlegenheit durch 15 Siege bei insgesamt 17 Rennen im Programm.

Ein überragendes Ergebnis, das einer Eintragung im Guinessbuch der Rekorde würdig ist. Schumachers persönliche Statistik bei dieser WM ist beeindruckend. Der Champion aus Kerpen fährt zehn Mal als Erster durchs Ziel, landet in allen Rennen auf dem Podium, und der dritte Platz im Grand Prix von Malaysia ist seine schlechteste Leistung dieser Saison. Schumacher übertrifft seinen Rekord von 2001, indem er durch den Sieg im Grand Prix von Frankreich schon sechs Runden vor Ende der Saison rechnerisch den Titel gewinnt und damit den historischen Rekord von 5 Titeln einstellt, den Juan Manuel Fangios für die Ewigkeit aufgestellt zu haben schien. Der Verdienst geht sicher auf Schumachers Klasse zurück und natürlich auf den F2002, den besten Ferrari aller Zeiten in der Formel 1 und wahrscheinlich sogar einen der innovativsten und wettbewerbsfähigsten Grand-Prix-Rennwagen der Geschichte.

2002

Ferrari surprised everyone by starting the 2002 season with the previous year's car while the revolutionary new F2002 was completed. The result stayed the same however with the red cars dominating qualifying for the Australian GP and the German taking an unrivalled victory. This was the start of a record-breaking world championship for the Ferrari-Schumacher pairing: the German confirmed himself to be the best driver in Formula 1 and the Italian cars proved to be superior than all the opposition by winning 15 out of the 17 races on the calendar.

Schumacher's record-breaking results make impressive reading: the German was first across the line on ten occasions, he finished on the podium in every race and third place in the Malaysian GP was his worst result of the year. Moreover, Schumacher improved on his 2001 record by mathematically clinching the title during the French GP, with six rounds left to be held, while equalling Juan Manuel Fangio's record of five world titles that seemed destined to last for ever.

This was clearly due to a combination of Schumacher's class and the performance of the F2002, the best F1 Ferrari of all time and probably one of the most innovative and competitive cars in Grand Prix history.

vodafone
Marlboro
Shell
BRIDGESTONE
AMD
vodafone
Alenia
brembo
MAHLE
vodafone

Die WM 2002 beginnt dramatisch, als in Australien der Ferrari von Barrichello mit dem Williams von Ralf Schumacher kollidiert und Michael dem Sieg entgegenfährt.

The 2002 championship started in a dramatic way when Barrichello's Ferrari landed on Ralf Schumacher's Williams in Australia and brother Michael took the win.

Schumacher und
sein Ferrari F2002
vernichten die
Konkurrenz. Nach
dem Debüt in
Brasilien
wiederholt der
Deutsche seinen
Sieg in Imola
(seitlich, und auf
dem Podium mit
Barrichello).

*Schumacher and
his Ferrari F2002
annihilated the
opposition. After
its debut in Brazil,
the German
driver repeated
the win at Imola
(alongside and
on the podium
with Barrichello).*

136

"Das Phänomen"
studiert die Zeiten
seiner Rivalen,
bevor er am Steuer
des Ferrari auf die
Piste geht. Auf den
folgenden Seiten
die technischen
Geheimnisse des
F2002.

"The Phenomenon"
studies the times
of his rivals before
going out on the
track in his Ferrari.
On the following
pages, the
technical secrets
of the F2002.

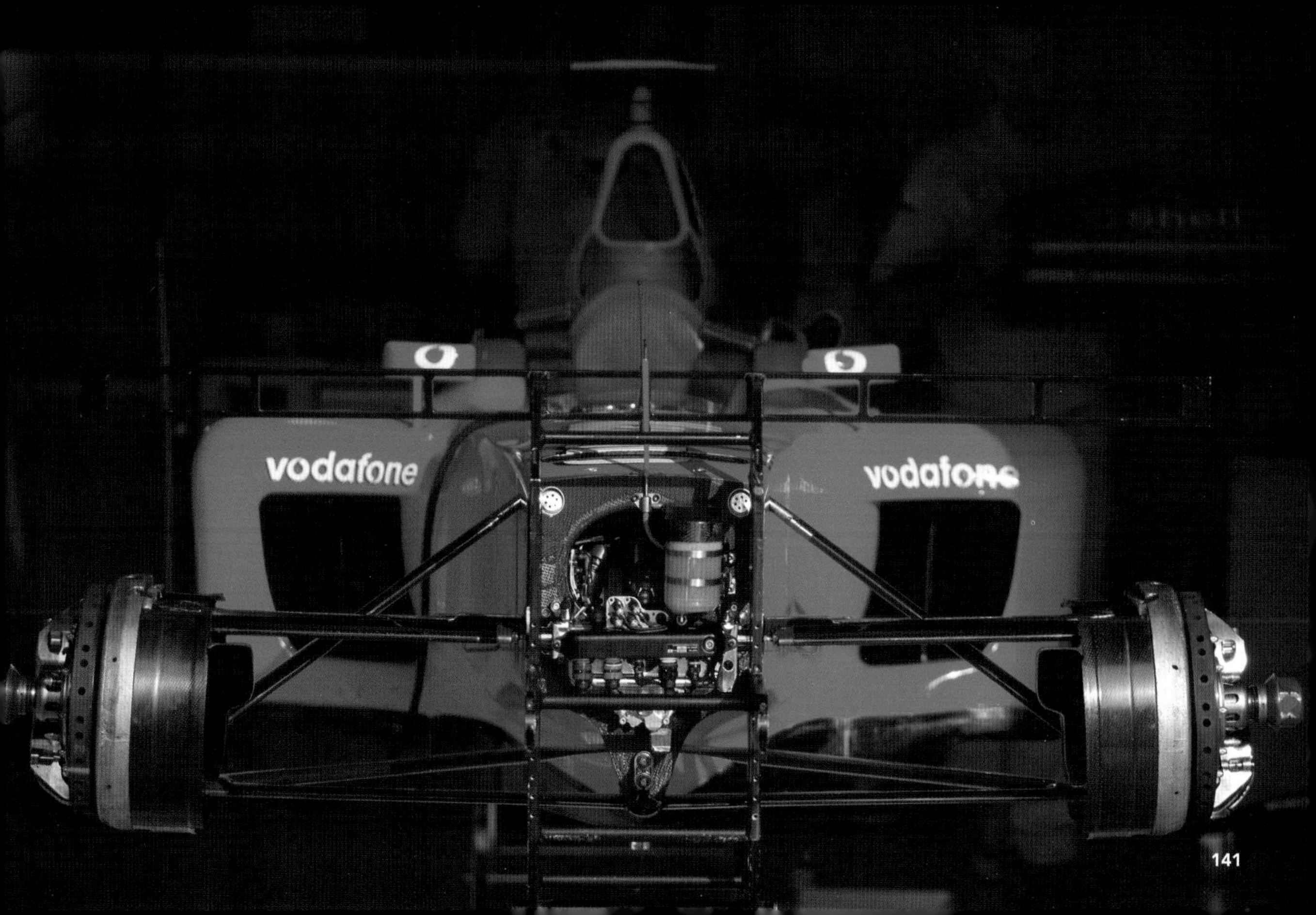
vodafone
vodafone

142

In der Weltmeister-
schaft der Rekorde
schlägt Schumacher
alle Rekorde mit
144 Punkten,
doppelt so viele wie
sein Teamkollege
Barrichello.

*Schumacher broke
all existing records
in his successful
2002 season. With
144 points to his
name, he scored
twice as many as
team-mate
Barrichello.*

144

Im Jahr 2002 erfolgte der Sieg mit mathematischer Bestimmtheit in Frankreich, sechs Rennen vor Ende der Saison (folgende Seiten).

In 2002 mathematical certainty of the title came in France, six rounds before the end of the season (following pages).

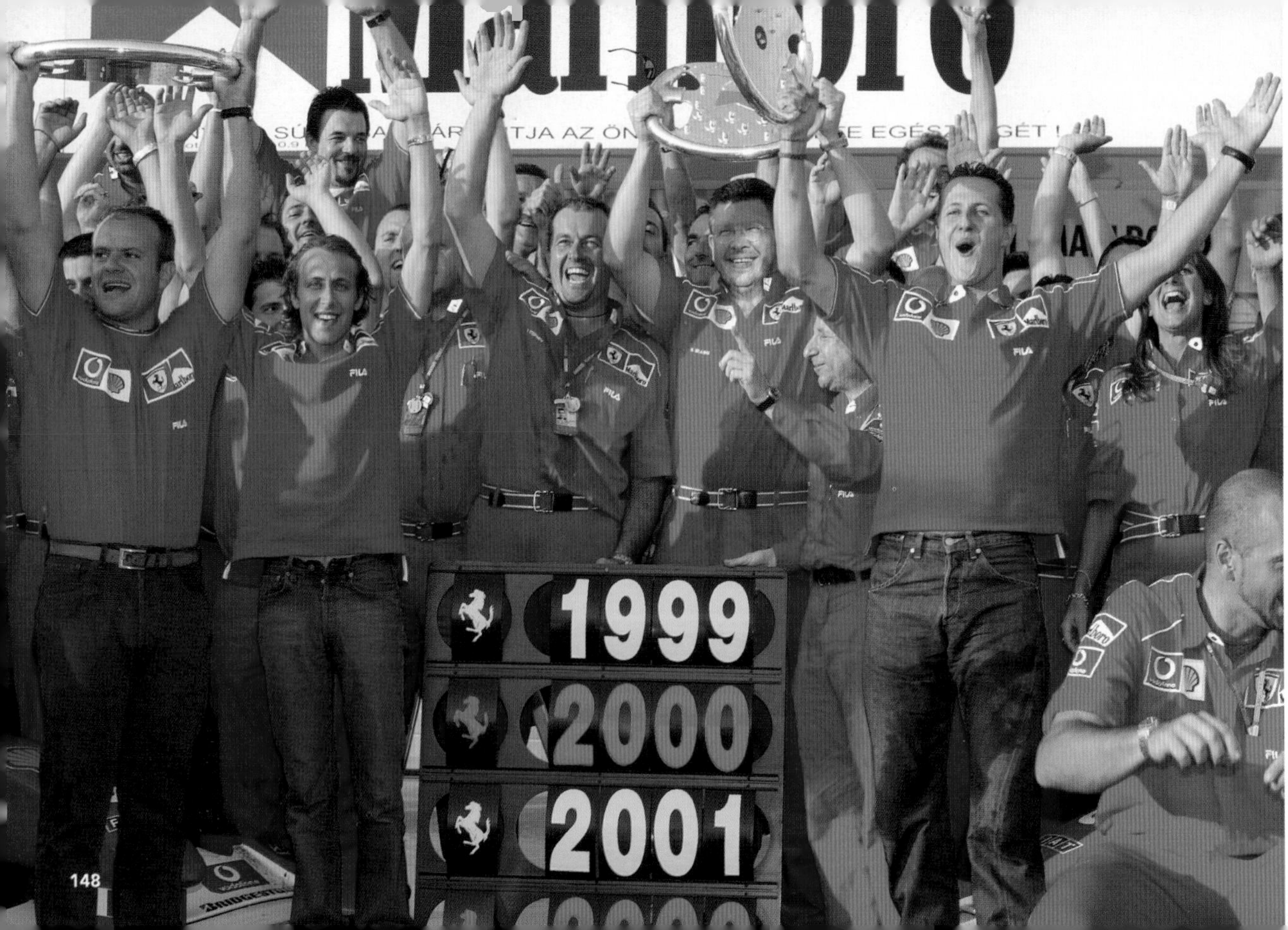
1999
2000
2001

Einen großen Verdienst an Michael Schumachers triumphaler Saison hat der erstaunliche Ferrari F2002.

A major contribution to Michael Schumacher's triumphant season came from the surprising Ferrari F2002.

Die technische
Überlegenheit
des Ferrari F2002
beweist sich
auch darin, dass
Rubens Barrichello
2002 Vize-Welt-
meister und Sieger
von fünf Grand
Prix wird.

*The technical
superiority of the
Ferrari F2002 was
also demonstrated
by Rubens
Barrichello, who
finished runner-up
to Schumacher
with five GP
wins to his name
in 2002.*

FERRARI F2002

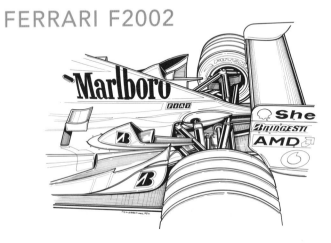

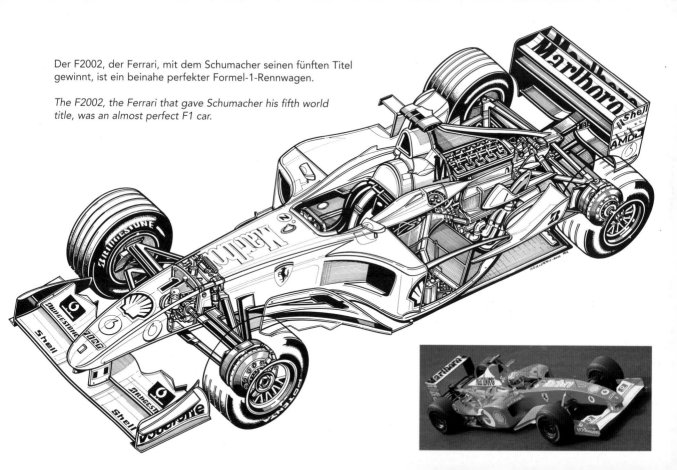

Der F2002, der Ferrari, mit dem Schumacher seinen fünften Titel gewinnt, ist ein beinahe perfekter Formel-1-Rennwagen.

The F2002, the Ferrari that gave Schumacher his fifth world title, was an almost perfect F1 car.

Wenn der Titel von 1994 der umstrittenste von Michael Schumachers Karriere ist, so ist der von 2003 zweifellos der am härtesten erkämpfte und der am schwersten erlangte. Den Prognosen vor der Saison zum Trotz, nach denen er eindeutig als Favorit galt, tut sich das Duo Schumacher-Ferrari zum Jahresbeginn schwer und muss auf den Grand Prix von Imola warten, dem vierten Rennen der Saison, um den ersten Sieg des "Phänomens" zu feiern. In Imola findet die kämpferische Karriere des F2002 ihren glorreichen Abschluss, aber auf dem Podium wird nicht gefeiert: Am Vorabend des Rennens starb die Mutter von Ralf und Michael Schumacher. Nach dem Überwinden der Anlaufschwierigkeiten kehrt Ferrari mit dem Debüt des F2003 GA, der Gianni Agnelli gewidmet ist, an die Spitze zurück.

Schumacher gewinnt in Spanien, Österreich und Kanada und wird Dritter in Monaco; man spricht wieder von der Vorherrschaft der Roten. Aber mit den Sommerrennen beginnt für seinen Ferrari und insbesondere für die Bridgestone Reifen des F2003 GA eine Krisenzeit. Während Williams, McLaren und Renault mit Michelin Bereifung in der Hitze zu fliegen scheinen, wird das "Cavallino"-Team gezwungen in die Defensive zu gehen, um den Schaden zu begrenzen. Die große Wende kommt in Monza. Die neue Bridgestone-Bereifung für den Grand Prix von Italien verleiht dem Ferrari und Schumacher Flügel, und aus der Pole Position heraus siegt er wohlverdient in einem der härtesten Rennen seiner Karriere. Zwei Wochen später schafft er dies nochmals in Indianapolis. In einem wegen des Regens halsbrecherischen Rennen, gewinnt er den sechsten Weltmeistertitel seiner Karriere.

While the 1994 title was the most controversial in Michael Schumacher's career, the 2003 crown was certainly the most hard-fought and the one where he faced the toughest opposition. Despite the pre-season pundits who put him as favourite, the Schumacher-Ferrari pairing stuttered to get off the mark at the start of the year and had to wait until the fourth round of the championship at Imola to score their first victory.

The San Marino Grand Prix brought an end to the glorious Formula 1 career of the F2002, but there were no celebrations on the podium due to the passing away of Michael and Ralf's mother the evening before the race. After overcoming its initial running-in period, Ferrari returned to the top with the brand-new F2003 GA, the car dedicated to the late Gianni Agnelli.

After Schumacher won in Spain, Austria and in Canada and was third at Monte Carlo, it looked as if the Italian cars were back to their usual dominant form. But with the summer races his Ferrari and above all the Bridgestone tyres on his F2003 GA started to enter a period of crisis. While Williams, McLaren and Renault, all on Michelin rubber, powered to the wins, the Prancing Horse team was forced into a defensive role to limit the damage. The turnaround came at Monza. The new Bridgestone tyres for the Italian Grand Prix helped Ferrari and after setting pole position, Schumacher took a well-deserved win in one of the toughest races of his career.

A fortnight later he repeated the result at Indianapolis, in a clamorous rain-affected race, which virtually gave him the sixth world title of his career.

Nach dem Sieg in Imola wird der F2002 in den Ruhestand geschickt und durch den F2003 GA ersetzt. Schumacher dominiert und gewinnt in Spanien (vorige Seite) und in Österreich (rechts).

After the win at Imola the F2002 was pensioned off and replaced by the F2003 GA. Schumacher dominated, winning in Spain (previous page) and in Austria (alongside).

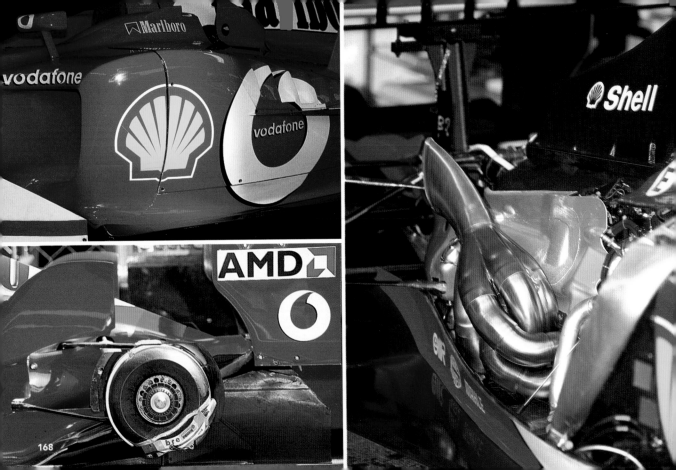

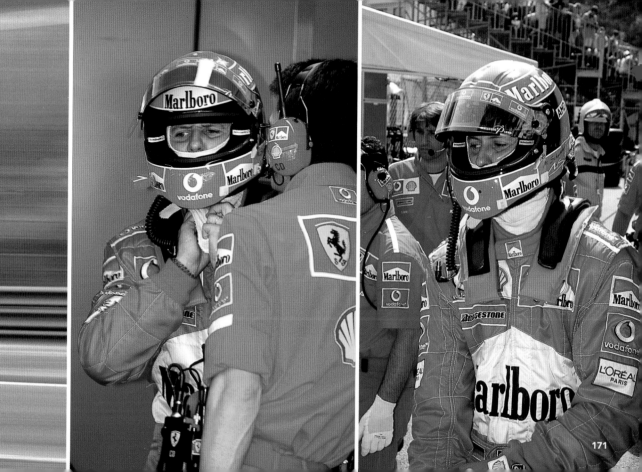

In den Sommer-
rennen muss
Schumi sich vor
dem Angriff von
Williams (rechts),
McLaren und
Renault mit ihren
jeweiligen Fahrern
verteidigen:
Räikkönen,
Montoya, Ralf
Schumacher und
Fernando Alonso
(folgende Seiten).

In the summer
races Schumy had
to defend himself
from the attacks
of Williams
(alongside),
McLaren and
Renault and their
respective drivers:
Montoya,
Ralf Schumacher,
Raikkonen and
Fernando Alonso
(following pages).

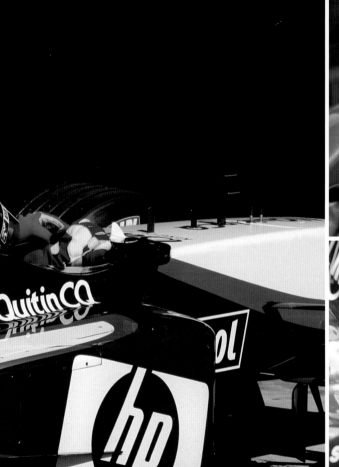

177

Mit dem Titel im Jahr 2003 ist Michael Schumacher der erfolgreichste Rennfahrer aller Zeiten.

With the 2003 title Michael Schumacher became the most successful driver of all time.

FERRARI F2003 GA

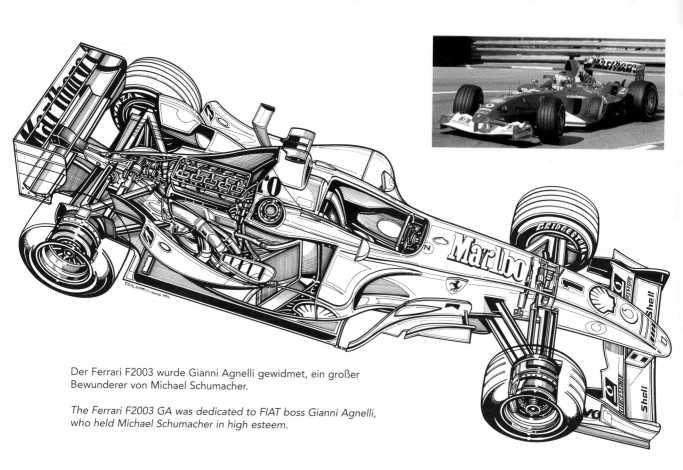

Der Ferrari F2003 wurde Gianni Agnelli gewidmet, ein großer
Bewunderer von Michael Schumacher.

*The Ferrari F2003 GA was dedicated to FIAT boss Gianni Agnelli,
who held Michael Schumacher in high esteem.*

Grand Prix Siege
Grand Prix Victories

1992	Spa-Francorchamps	30.8.1992	Benetton-Ford 192
1993	Estoril	26.9.1993	Benetton-Ford 194
1994	San Paolo	27.3.1994	Benetton-Ford 194
	Aida	17.4.1994	Benetton-Ford 194
	Imola	1.5.1994	Benetton-Ford 194
	Montecarlo	15.5.1994	Benetton-Ford 194
	Montreal	27.3.1994	Benetton-Ford 194
	Magny Cours	3.7.1994	Benetton-Ford 194
	Hungaroring	15.5.1994	Benetton-Ford 194
	Jerez	27.3.1994	Benetton-Ford 194
1995	San Paolo	26.3.1995	Benetton-Ford 195
	Catalunya	14.5.1995	Benetton-Ford 195
	Montecarlo	28.5.1995	Benetton-Ford 195
	Magny Cours	2.7.1995	Benetton-Ford 195
	Hockenheim	30.7.1995	Benetton-Ford 195
	Spa-Francorchamps	27.8.1995	Benetton-Ford 195
	Nürburgring	1.10.1995	Benetton-Ford 195
	Aida	22.10.1995	Benetton-Ford 195
	Suzuka	29.10.1995	Benetton-Ford 195

1996	Catalunya	2.6.1996	Ferrari F310
	Spa-Francorchamps	25.8.1996	Ferrari F310
	Monza	8.9.1996	Ferrari F310
1997	Montecarlo	11.7.1997	Ferrari F310B
	Montreal	15.6.1997	Ferrari F310B
	Magny Cours	11.7.1997	Ferrari F310B
	Spa-Francorchamps	24.8.1997	Ferrari F310B
	Suzuka	11.7.1997	Ferrari F310B
1998	Buenos Aires	12.4.1998	Ferrari F300
	Montreal	7.6.1998	Ferrari F300
	Magny Cours	28.6.1998	Ferrari F300
	Hungaroring	16.8.1998	Ferrari F300
	Monza	13.9.1998	Ferrari F300
1999	Imola	5.5.1999	Ferrari F399
	Montecarlo	16.5.1999	Ferrari F399
2000	Melbourne	12.3.2000	Ferrari F1 2000
	Interlagos	26.3.2000	Ferrari F1 2000
	Imola	9.4.2000	Ferrari F1 2000
	Nürburgring	21.5.2000	Ferrari F1 2000
	Montreal	18.6.2000	Ferrari F1 2000
	Monza	10.9.2000	Ferrari F1 2000
	Indianapolis	24.9.2000	Ferrari F1 2000
	Suzuka	8.10.2000	Ferrari F1 2000
	Sepang	22.10.2000	Ferrari F1 2000

2001	Melbourne	4.3.2001	Ferrari F2001
	Sepang	18.3.2001	Ferrari F2001
	Jerez	29.4.2001	Ferrari F2001
	Montecarlo	27.5.2001	Ferrari F2001
	Nürburgring	4.3.2001	Ferrari F2001
	Magny Cours	1.7.2001	Ferrari F2001
	Hungaroring	19.8.2001	Ferrari F2001
	Spa-Francorchamps	2.9.2001	Ferrari F2001
	Suzuka	14.10.2001	Ferrari F2001
2002	Melbourne	3.3.2002	Ferrari F2001
	Interlagos	31.3.2002	Ferrari F2002
	Imola	14.4.2002	Ferrari F2002
	Catalunya	28.4.2002	Ferrari F2002
	Zeltweg	12.5.2002	Ferrari F2002
	Montreal	9.6.2002	Ferrari F2002
	Silverstone	7.7.2002	Ferrari F2002
	Magny Cours	21.7.2002	Ferrari F2002
	Hockenheim	28.7.2002	Ferrari F2002
	Spa-Francorchamps	1.9.2002	Ferrari F2002
	Suzuka	13.10.2002	Ferrari F2002
2003	Imola	20.4.2003	Ferrari F2002
	Catalunya	28.4.2003	Ferrari F2003 GA
	Zeltweg	18.5.2003	Ferrari F2003 GA
	Montreal	15.6.2003	Ferrari F2003 GA
	Monza	14.9.2003	Ferrari F2003 GA
	Indianapolis	28.9.2003	Ferrari F2003 GA

Paolo D'Alessio wird 1957 in der Provinz von Turin geboren und beginnt 1978 sich mit dem Motorsport zu beschäftigen. Er arbeitet mit einigen Fachzeitschriften zusammen und fängt an die Formel 1 zu verfolgen, insbesondere in Hinblick auf die technische Weiterentwicklung der Grand-Prix-Rennwagen. Seine Artikel, ausgestattet mit detaillierten Zeichnungen, werden in den führenden Fachmagazinen und Sportzeitungen der ganzen Welt veröffentlicht. Zurzeit arbeitet er mit ca. zwanzig Zeitschriften und Sportzeitungen zusammen. Sein erstes Buch erscheint 1985 und handelt von Ferrari und seinen Turbo-Rennwagen. Von 1986 bis 1994 ist er für das internationale Jahrbuch '365 Racing Days' verantwortlich und seit 1995, für die bekannteste und in der ganzen Welt verbreitete Sonderausgabe über die Formel 1, herausgegeben vom Verlag S.E.P. Editrice. Weitere veröffentlichte Bücher sind 'Formula 1 turbo', 'Obrigado Ayrton', dem unvergesslichen Ayrton Senna gewidmet, 'Kaiser Schumy', 'Martini Racing Story' und 'Formula Ferrari', das vollständigste Werk, das je über Ferrari-Rennwagen herausgegeben wurde. 1987 realisiert er zusammen mit Momo Design eine Reihe von Lithografien, die den 40 Jahren von Ferrari in der Formel 1 gewidmet sind, und kürzlich eine Briefmarkenenzyklopädie von Ferrari, herausgegeben von Bolaffi. 1997 signiert er den Pokal der Honda Trophy, das Symbol des japanischen Herstellers in Motorsport-Wettkämpfen und öffentlichen Veranstaltungen.

Paolo D'Alessio was born in the province of Turin in 1957, Paolo D'Alessio first became involved in motorsport in 1978. He collaborated with several specialised publications and began to follow Formula 1, in particular the technical developments of Grand Prix cars. His articles, together with his detailed cutaway designs, are published in the leading specialised magazines and sports daily newspapers throughout the world. He currently collaborates with about 20 publications and newspapers. His first book dates back to 1985 and the subject was Ferrari and its turbo-charged cars. From 1986 to 1994 he was responsible for the international yearbook 365 Racing Days and, starting from 1995, the special yearbook on Formula 1, published by S.E.P. Editrice, which has become the most well-known and widespread book on F1 throughout the world. His other published books include Formula 1 turbo, Obrigado Ayrton (dedicated to the legendary Ayrton Senna), Kaiser Schumy, Martini Racing Story and Formula Ferrari, the most complete work dedicated to Ferrari racing cars. In 1987, together with Momo Design, he produced a collection of lithograph prints, dedicated to 40 years of Ferrari in Formula 1, and the recent Ferrari stamp-collecting encyclopaedia, for Bolaffi. In 1997 he put his signature to the Honda Trophy, the symbol of the Japanese manufacturer in motorsport competition and public events.